An introduction to supporting people with autistic spectrum conditions

Series Editor: Lesley Barcham

Mandatory unit and Common Induction Standards titles

Communicating effectively with people with a learning disability
ISBN 978 0 85725 510 5

Personal development for learning disability workers ISBN 978 0 85725 609 6

Equality and inclusion for learning disability workers ISBN 978 0 85725 514 3

Duty of care for learning disability workers ISBN 978 0 85725 613 3

Principles of safeguarding and protection for learning disability workers
ISBN 978 0 85725 506 8

Person centred approaches when supporting people with a learning disability
ISBN 978 0 85725 625 6

The role of the learning disability worker ISBN 978 0 85725 637 9

Handling information for learning disability workers ISBN 978 0 85725 633 1

Titles supporting a unit from the level 2 health and social care qualifications

An introduction to supporting people with autistic spectrum conditions
ISBN 978 0 85725 710 7

An introduction to supporting people with autistic spectrum conditions

Sue Hatton and Tom Boughton

Supporting a unit from the level 2 health and
social care qualifications

all about people

Acknowledgements

Photographs from www.shutterstock.com and www.careimages.com. Our thanks to Sue Hatton, Tom Boughton, Alex and John, and to Choices Housing for their help.

First published in 2011 jointly by Learning Matters Ltd and the British Institute of Learning Disabilities

British Library Cataloguing in Publication Data
A CIP record for this book is available from the British Library

ISBN: 978 0 85725 701 7

This book is also available in the following ebook formats:
Adobe ebook ISBN: 978 0 85725 635 5
ePUB ebook ISBN: 978 0 85725 634 8
Kindle ISBN: 978 0 85725 636 2

The rights of Sue Hatton and Tom Boughton to be identified as the authors of this Work have been asserted by them in accordance with the Copyright, Designs and Patents Act 1988.

Cover design by Pentacor
Text design by Pentacor
Project Management by Deer Park Productions
Typeset by Pantek Media, Maidstone
Printed and bound in Great Britain by Ashford Colour Press Ltd, Gosport, Hants

Learning Matters Ltd
20 Cathedral Yard
Exeter
EX1 1HB
Tel: 01392 215560
E-mail: info@learningmatters.co.uk
www.learningmatters.co.uk

BILD
Campion House
Green Street
Kidderminster
Worcestershire
DY10 1JL
Tel: 01562 723010
E-mail: enquiries@bild.org.uk
www.bild.org.uk

Contents

This book covers:

- The Level 2 health and social care unit LD 210 – Introductory awareness of autistic spectrum conditions

About the authors and the people who contributed to this book

Sue Hatton and Tom Boughton

Sue Hatton is a teacher by training and worked in schools and then two further education colleges. It was here that she first met Tom Boughton, who was a 16 year old with autism in her tutor group. Together they began a journey to understand the impact of autism on Tom's life and what could best be done to support Tom effectively in his learning, and also to enable him in his adult life. Tom discovered that finding out about his own autism helped him to make sense of his experiences in life, and it also led to the development of a new skill – an ability to help others understand autism.

In the last 16 years Sue has worked for an autism specific charity as their learning and development manager. She now works as an autism adviser for a national company that runs specialist education and health and social care services.

Sue has a master's degree with a special study in autistic spectrum conditions and has co-authored another BILD book with a woman with Asperger syndrome, *Conversations in Autism – from insight to good practice*.

The quest for a better understanding of autistic spectrum conditions continues as new insights come to life when Sue and Tom are working on the preparation of a new piece of training, or indeed as they worked together on the material for this book.

Several people have made contributions to this book and Sue and Tom are grateful for their honesty and willingness to share their stories to help others gain a better understanding of autistic spectrum conditions.

Vivien Boughton

Tom's mum, who speaks about the growing awareness she and her family have that autism affects not just the individual who gets the diagnosis but the whole family.

Alex

A young man with autism who was extremely challenging when Sue taught him. Eventually he was willing to go on the same journey of discovery as Tom, and like Tom is now able to help others understand.

John

John was educated in a mainstream school but he found himself a patient in an adolescent psychiatric unit before he got his diagnosis of Asperger Syndrome. John's insight into his own autistic spectrum condition, and that of those he supports as a part time care worker in a residential service for people with autism, is extremely valuable and greatly contributes to the understanding of autism as a spectrum condition.

Elizabeth and Linda

Elizabeth and Linda are friends and ex-colleagues of Sue, both of whom have a son with autism and severe learning disabilities. Their ability to tell their, at times, painful story and the continuing journey they are on remains a guiding light for all the work Sue does in the field of autistic spectrum conditions.

Naomi Owereh

Naomi brought her own knowledge and understanding of autistic spectrum conditions to bear on the editing process and her commitment to the project is much appreciated.

Introduction

Who is this book for?

An Introduction to Supporting People with Autistic Spectrum Conditions is for you if you:

- want an introduction to providing a service to or supporting people with autism;

- are a worker or volunteer in an organisation such as a college, leisure centre community or health centre and you occasionally provide services to people with an autistic spectrum condition;

- work in health or social care with people with autism or people with a learning disability who also have autism;

- are a manager in a service supporting people with autistic spectrum conditions or people with a learning disability and autism and you have training or supervisory responsibility for the development of your staff;

- are a direct payment or personal budget user and are planning learning opportunities for your personal assistant.

Links to qualifications

This book gives you all the information you need to complete the level 2 unit, *Introductory awareness of autistic spectrum conditions*, from the level 2 diploma in health and social care, as well as the level 2 learning disability certificate and award. You may use the learning from this book to:

- work towards a full qualification, e.g. the level 2 diploma in health and social care;

- achieve accreditation for a single unit on autism awareness.

Although anyone studying for the qualifications will find the book useful, it is particularly helpful for people who provide services to or who support a person with autism. The messages and stories used in this book are from people with an autistic spectrum condition, family carers and people working with them.

Links to assessment

If you are studying for this unit and want to gain accreditation towards a qualification, first of all you will need to make sure that you are registered with an awarding organisation who offers the qualification. Then you will need to provide a portfolio of evidence for assessment. The person responsible for training within your organisation will advise you about registering with an awarding organisation and give you information about the type of evidence you will need to provide for assessment. You can also get additional information from BILD. For more information about qualifications and assessment, go to the BILD website: www.bild.org.uk/qualifications

How this book is organised

Generally each chapter covers one learning outcome from the qualification unit *introductory awareness of autistic spectrum conditions*. The learning outcomes covered are clearly highlighted at the beginning of each chapter. Each chapter starts with a story from a person with autism or family carer or worker. This introduces the topic and is intended to help you think about the topic from their point of view. Each chapter contains:

Thinking points – to help you reflect on your practice;

Stories – examples of good support from people with learning disabilities and family carers;

Activities – for you to use to help you to think about your work with people with learning disabilities;

Key points – a summary of the main messages in that chapter;

References and where to go for more information – useful references to help further study.

At the end of the book there is:

A glossary – explaining specialist language in plain English;

An index – to help you look up a particular topic easily.

Study skills

Studying for a qualification can be very rewarding. However, it can be daunting if you have not studied for a long time, or are wondering how to fit your studies into an already busy life. The BILD website contains lots of advice to help you to study successfully, including information about effective reading, taking notes, organising your time, and using the internet for research. For further information, go to www.bild.org.uk/qualifications

Chapter 1

Understanding autism

> People need to understand **MY** autism if they are going to support me.
>
> *Tom – a person with autism*

Introduction

If you ever get the opportunity to listen to someone with autism speaking about their life, take it. You will learn things from them which no textbook can teach. Several people with autism have written about their feelings and experiences. A few examples are given in the references at the end of this chapter and it is recommended that you read one or more of these. Tom, quoted above, has been involved in writing this book and throughout you will read about his experiences of living with autism. Tom's mother has also been interviewed and has made a valuable contribution in sharing her understanding of autism, and the impact it has had on her son and upon family life. Tom's and his mother's accounts provide invaluable insights. However, it is important to remember that autism affects people in different ways. The thoughts and experiences of a range of individuals with autism are included within this book to give you a broad perspective.

Learning outcomes

This chapter will help you to:

- understand why it is important to recognise that each person on the autistic spectrum has their own individual abilities, needs, strengths, preferences and interests;

- understand the types of difficulties that individuals with an autistic spectrum condition may have with language and communicating with others;

- identify problems that individuals with an autistic spectrum condition may have in social interaction and relationships;

- understand the problems of inflexibility and restrictiveness in activities and interests and how these may affect individuals on the autistic spectrum;

- recognise the sensory difficulties experienced by many individuals with autistic spectrum conditions;

- identify other conditions which may be associated with autistic spectrum conditions;

- understand why autism can be considered as a spectrum, such that individuals differ in the expression and severity of their symptoms.

This chapter covers:

Level 2 LD 210 – Introductory awareness of autistic spectrum conditions: Learning Outcomes 1 and 2

A word about language

Language is developing all the time, and the words we use to describe a particular impairment or disability change as a result of listening to people with personal experience, as a result of changing values and attitudes in society and as a result of new research. The terminology used to describe the autistic spectrum has changed over time. The terminology used in this book to describe the autistic spectrum is autistic spectrum conditions (ASC); this is one of several common usages at the time of writing. The term autistic spectrum disorder is still used sometimes in more clinical or research settings. The term autism is often used, and is still widely accepted, as an umbrella term for the spectrum, for example by organisations such as the National Autistic Society. Autistic spectrum conditions has been chosen for this book as it is a more neutral and less medical term than autistic spectrum disorder. When you are working with a person with autism listen to the words they and their family use to describe their condition and then if you are comfortable take your lead from them.

Individual abilities, needs, strengths, preferences and interests

Autism is a developmental disability. This means that it arises in infancy or early childhood, and results in the delayed development of abilities such as language and play with others. Autism affects every aspect of an individual for the entire length of their life, especially their communication, social interaction, ways of thinking and behaving and their senses.

It is also important to remember that each person with autism is an individual, having their own personality, their own family and community culture. In order to be truly person centred we need to be aware of every aspect of who they are and learn to value what is important to them, no matter how strange or unusual it may be to us. For example, one person that I know with an autistic spectrum condition is extremely interested in windows and he loves to talk about the different kinds of windows you can find in buildings. Being willing to both listen and share in this interest is a key way of giving this person both respect and acceptance. This is equally true for someone with more severe learning disabilities and autism who may enjoy more than anything else sifting sand. Not only is it important to allow this to happen and encourage what they enjoy to really show a sense of value, it is also worth sharing the experience. This may sound a little strange, and of course we should not just leave an individual sifting sand all day, but there is something about valuing what they value if we are to be person centred.

The triad of impairments and sensory difficulties

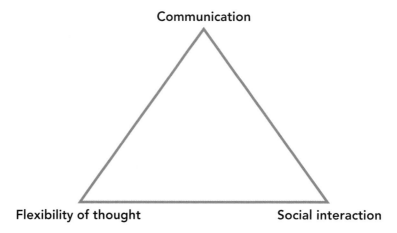

The triad of impairments.

For many years it has been understood that when autism is diagnosed three main areas of difficulty are evident. These are:

- problems with social interaction and relationships;
- difficulties with language and communication;
- problems with ways of thinking.

These have traditionally been referred to as the 'triad of impairments'. In addition, it is now increasingly understood that people with autism experience their senses very differently to others and this also needs to be considered when offering support.

Before we examine these four areas of autism in more depth, there are three points on which you should be clear:

1. Autism is a spectrum of conditions. It has different effects on different people. Although all people with autism share certain characteristics, they are individuals and must be treated as such. Working in a person centred way is important and will be explored fully in Chapter 4. To do this for someone with autism we have to understand *their* autism.

2. The model of the triad of impairments is still widely used to understand autism and it is extremely important to know the impact of each area within the triad. But do not underestimate the impact of sensory issues for every person with autistic spectrum conditions.

3. In your experience of providing a service to, or supporting, a person with autism, taking a positive and person centred approach is paramount.

Whilst autism leads to some difficulties and challenges, equally it is vital to recognise an individual's gifts and abilities and once again to value them and use them if you are to be truly person centred. If someone is very tidy and likes to make sure everything is in its place, involve them in the housework. If someone is good with bus numbers and bus routes give them responsibility for teaching new staff the best bus routes to different places. People with autism have much to offer and you need to support the person you work with to know you appreciate their gifts and skills.

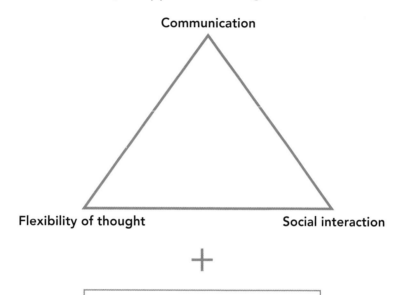

The triad of impairments and sensory difficulties.

Tom's mum was asked if the diagnosis of autism was helpful for Tom and for them as a family. Her reply was:

At the time I was looking for a solution, a way of preventing what felt like the loss of Tom's childhood, but now I think the diagnosis is a protection.

A diagnosis of autistic spectrum conditions is usually only given after detailed observation and interviews with the individual themselves, if possible, as well as parents and other significant people in the life of the individual. A doctor with specialist knowledge about autistic spectrum conditions is most likely to do this. They often involve other professionals such as a speech and language therapist, teacher or psychologist.

Let's now look more closely at the 'triad of impairments' and the sensory difficulties people might experience.

Social interaction and relationships

Not being able to relate socially to other people is a major defining characteristic of autism. This can take a number of forms:

- not paying any attention to others, being aloof, seeming distant or uninterested;
- giving an impression of aloneness, being withdrawn, and retreating into a shell;
- a lack of social skills, inappropriate eye contact or laughter, not understanding about friendship or strangers, saying things or behaving in ways not suitable for the circumstances;
- appearing very self centred and unaware or uncaring about others;
- being over friendly and familiar with people.

> *Tom's mum says:*
>
> Tom is very passive, he likes to have plans to meet people who he calls friends, but once they have met and had the cup of coffee or lunch then Tom is keen to get away again.

Language and communication

People who have autism will have difficulties with communication, although it may not seem obvious if they speak and use language. It is the two-way, give and take of how we communicate with each other that people with autism struggle with. Difficulties with language and communication may be shown in the following ways:

- Some children with autism never develop meaningful speech, but still understand things that are said to them and around them.

- Some children develop what appear to be good language skills, but their ability to really understand what is said to them is very poor.

- Individuals may not speak and yet understand a lot of what is said to them. Others may speak but this masks the fact they do not fully understand what they are saying.

- There may be an inability to properly read non-verbal communication, such as tone of voice, facial expressions, body posture, and gestures like pointing. Non-verbal communication like this is key to relationships and not understanding it can cause huge difficulties for the individual.

- Problems can arise from patterns of speech commonly used in early childhood development which continue into later life. Examples include: parroting what people say; making up words; talking constantly about one subject; and having difficulty using pronouns such as 'I' and 'you' correctly.

Tom says:

I need time to think when people speak to me if I am going to understand what they say.

People with autism often need extra time to understand what is said to them.

Problems with ways of thinking

People with autism can often have significant difficulty in understanding how other people think, feel and react. Not appreciating what other people are thinking can lead them to speak and act in ways which seem strange. It can also mean that people with autistic spectrum conditions can get confused by what others say and do. People with autism tend to be quite self absorbed in their own thoughts and behaviour patterns. They don't mean to be selfish or self centred but it is the nature of the disability that they can appear like this.

The behaviour of people with autism tends to share certain characteristics, including:

- liking repetitive patterns of sound or behaviour;
- a tendency to be rigid and obsessive;
- limited use of imagination;
- resistance to change and a dislike of variety;
- a real need for predictability;
- a particular and special interest in one or two things.

> *Tom says:*
>
> It makes me feel calm and happy when things stay the same and are predictable. I find change difficult.

Sensory difficulties experienced by people with an autistic spectrum condition

To begin to understand the sensory differences for people with autism we have to first grasp that, in addition to the usual five senses (hearing, seeing, taste, touch and smell), we also have a vestibular sense and a proprioceptive sense. Vestibular sense is our sense of balance. Proprioceptive sense is how we know where we are in space, for example how we are able to judge getting through a doorway when carrying a large object. Our brains and bodies are processing things in a sensory way all the time. When we come into a room we are aware if it is dark or cold, crowded or damp, without really being conscious of making these judgements. We can respond appropriately by putting a light on or doing up our coat. People with autism struggle to process their sensory experience in the same way and at the same speed as others. Some people with autism have a severely reduced ability to respond in an appropriate sensory way. Donna Williams, author of *Nobody, Nowhere*, refers to herself as being 'mono channelled'. Her sensory impairment means she can only process one sensory experience at a time.

Tom says:

There are lots of things I find difficult, looking at people in the face, background music in a pub, and the smells in people's houses. I cope better now I am older but I still find certain noises very frightening.

Tom's mum says:

There were occasions when Tom was a child that he experienced real sensory overload on entering a particular place – too much hitting his senses all at once. He couldn't deal with it, for example if we went to a children's party – we just had to go home.

You need to take account of and respond to these sensory issues as this is part of who each person with an autistic spectrum condition is. If you are to work in a person centred way then this includes taking seriously these sensory differences and difficulties and not making light of them. It also includes trying to work them out for those who are not able to tell us, but whose behaviour does let us know they are in distress.

People on the autistic spectrum are all different. This means one individual will respond to the experience of sensory overload by making lots of noise themselves and running around in a very overexcited way, which can lead to violent or aggressive behaviour. Other people with autism will withdraw into themselves and seem to be lost in deep concentration. Predictable patterns, as Tom told us earlier, are often calming. However, it is possible that a person might develop negative predictable patterns. It is important when supporting somebody with an autistic spectrum condition to try and help them establish positive predictability.

Activity

Think of somebody with autism you support or have supported. Divide a piece of paper into four. In each quarter write down one of the four characteristics of autism as a heading. Under these headings, describe how each area of autism is expressed in the individual you have chosen.

Autism as a spectrum and people's different experiences

Understanding the main characteristics of autistic spectrum conditions is not enough on its own as a basis for learning how to support people with autism effectively. You need also to be aware of the spectrum of autism, and of the range that can be found within it.

In thinking about a spectrum we need to consider the severity of the person's autism and also the nature of the individual's learning disability, if this is relevant. A learning disability includes the presence of a significantly reduced ability to understand new or complex information and to learn new skills together with a reduced ability to cope independently. A person's learning disability would start before adulthood, and it would have a lasting effect on their development.

The labels we attach to certain parts of the spectrum are a guide and do not indicate clear-cut boundaries between one condition and another. One form of autism tends to merge into another, and sometimes it can be unclear where on the spectrum an individual stands. This does not matter greatly, provided enough is understood about the person's needs to ensure that they receive all the necessary and appropriate support.

Learning disabilities can also be seen as a spectrum. Many people with autism, particularly those receiving support, will also have a learning disability. This may be anything from severe to mild in nature, merging at the mild end of the spectrum into that range of individuals who have an autistic condition, but no learning disability. These individuals will still have difficulty in the areas described previously and everyone with a diagnosis will need 'autism friendly' support, no matter where they are on the spectrum.

John is a man in his twenties who has Asperger syndrome. He is very keen for people to understand about the 'uneven cognitive profile' in autism. This means that an individual may have a severe learning disability and autism, and need help using the toilet and crossing the road, but the same individual is able to do a complex puzzle. John describes coming top in most of his lessons at his mainstream secondary school, but having no idea of how to make a friend or how to arrange to go to the cinema. The uneven cognitive profile is a difficult but absolutely essential concept to grasp. It helps us to stop making assumptions about what an individual with autism can or can't do.

> *Tom says:*
>
> People often think I am very able because I can catch a bus and get money from my bank account but there is so much I need help with, like how to make a choice. I find making choices difficult and stressful.
>
> *John echoes this difficulty with choices when he says:*
>
> I don't want to be told I **may** be able to go and watch Manchester United at the ground or I **may** watch it on TV at the sports club, I really don't mind which I do, but I do **NEED** to **know** which.

Thinking point

Consider something that surprises you about someone you know with autistic spectrum conditions. It could be something that they are very good at or that they really struggle with, but something that you find surprising. This will be another example of the uneven cognitive profile.

Key conditions on the autistic spectrum

We will now look at the main characteristics of some key conditions on the autistic spectrum:

- Classic or Kanner's autism;
- Pervasive developmental disorder not otherwise specified (PDD-NOS);
- High-functioning autism;
- Asperger syndrome.

Do not be put off by the fact that these labels appear to come from a medical model of autism, which focuses on diagnosing and treating an illness or condition. They are widely used and there is no reason why a label of autism cannot be a basis for organising holistic care and support based on a social model of disability. The social model of disability says that a person is disabled by the barriers in society. Many people with autism experience barriers because of people's attitude and prejudice towards them and their autism.

Classic autism

This is also referred to as **Kanner's autism** in recognition of the observations on the condition published by Leo Kanner in 1943. In classic autism:

- all three areas of the triad of impairments will be present as well as sensory processing difficulties;
- there will be difficulty with social interactions, including indifference to other people, one-sided interactions, and an inability to understand the reactions of others;
- problems will occur in social communication, such as not understanding tone of voice or facial expressions, or finding it hard to communicate by word or gesture;
- there will be limited imagination or rigidity in activities or pursuits, often combined with repetitive or obsessive approaches.

Pervasive developmental disorder not otherwise specified (PDD-NOS)

As mentioned at the start of this chapter, autism is itself a pervasive developmental disability. A pervasive disability is one that affects many areas of development. However, PDD-NOS is used where someone has severe and pervasive impairments in all three parts of the triad of impairments, but does not meet the criteria for a specific disorder.

Wendy Lawson, who has an autistic spectrum condition, points out that this may be no more than saying we do not know what is wrong. She expresses concern that a diagnosis of this kind may be confusing and unhelpful.

High-functioning autism

The usual, and useful, meaning of this description is that the person has an autism spectrum condition, but does not have a learning disability. Be aware that this term is sometimes used as if it had the same meaning as Asperger syndrome. It is essential to remember the uneven cognitive profile even when someone is very able or high functioning, as the individual may well surprise you by being very able and yet not grasping things that seem very obvious or simple.

> *John says:*
>
> I understand about the need to wash underwear and socks every day but I really don't understand how you know when to wash your trousers or a jumper.

Asperger syndrome

Asperger syndrome is a condition described by Hans Asperger in 1944; the year after Kanner published his observations. When later it was realised that people with Kanner's autism and Asperger syndrome have much in common, the term 'autism spectrum disorders' was coined. Now the term 'autism spectrum conditions' is also in use. If autism is seen as a continuum, Asperger syndrome is often described as close to, or merging into, high-functioning autism. Some people think they are the same thing and others feel it is important to make a distinction.

The areas which classic autism and Asperger syndrome have in common tend to be mapped to the main characteristics of autism:

- difficulties in social relationships;
- problems in communicating;
- poor ability with flexible thinking, not understanding what goes on in other people's heads and a need for predictability;
- sensory processing difficulties and differences.

There are also areas in which they differ. For a diagnosis of Asperger syndrome the person will have:

- normal development of speech and language, though will still have a problem with two-way communication;
- an absence of a learning disability (but will still have an uneven cognitive profile, as referred to by John earlier);
- an average or higher level of intelligence.

The conditions we have looked at are labels. They may be useful in ensuring that the right services and support are given to people with autism, but should never be allowed to detract from their individuality as human beings. The main characteristics of the autism spectrum should be used to enable you to appreciate the diversity of the people you support, and the range of their needs.

Other conditions associated with an autistic spectrum condition

It is quite common for people with an autism spectrum condition to have an additional condition. The National Autistic Society tells us that at least 70% of people who have autism also have an additional condition. For example, you may know a person with:

- autism and epilepsy;

- autism and bowel problems;

- autism and a restricted or very specific diet;

- an autistic spectrum condition and a mental health problem;

- autism and an additional genetic condition like Fragile X syndrome or Down's syndrome.

Ensuring individuals get really good support when their autism is combined with other conditions presents an even greater challenge. It is vital to really get to know the individual and think deeply about the complexity of their needs.

Activity

Write down the name of two people you know with autistic spectrum conditions. Which of the labels we have been exploring fits each individual best? Can you identify something about their 'uneven cognitive profile'?

How inflexibility and restrictiveness in activities may affect an individual on the autistic spectrum

What this usually means is behaviour which is odd or which causes difficulties. You should never forget that some behaviours exhibited by people with autism are strengths.

Consistency and predictability

This can be very positive in that it makes individuals very reliable and able to do tasks successfully for long periods of time that others would find boring. Predictability is crucial for people with autism. However, it is also our job as supporters to help people with autism learn to cope with change.

> *John says:*
>
> For me autism **IS** the quest for predictability, and that is why I like buses so much. I like the reliability of their numbers and routes, the bus stops and the garages they go to at night.

Single-mindedness

If you share a common interest with a person who has autism, this may make it relatively easy to talk to each other. From this start, it may be possible to build a relationship, which can be extended into other areas of communication and social contact.

> *Anne, from Tom's circle of support, says:*
>
> When Tom and I meet for coffee we always talk about what has been happening in the Archers. We are both fans of the Archers and it is really helpful that I share this special interest with Tom.

Focus

If someone with autism is interested in a subject, they will pay it careful attention. If you know about their special interest you can then use this as a starting point to support their learning.

> *John says:*
>
> I have no problem in busy train stations working out which train to catch and so on because I am totally focused on the information about the trains and I do not get side-tracked. People say they like travelling with me as they don't have to worry about the journey as they know I will know exactly what is happening all the time.

'Islets of special ability'

This refers to the way in which small numbers of people with autism develop a special talent, often early in life. This may be in one of the arts, or an aspect of science, or an activity such as putting together jigsaws. Such people may be unaware that their talent is special. The artist Stephen Wiltshire is one of the most famous people with autism in this country. He has a very special gift for drawing buildings and cityscapes. Exceptional talent like this is rare, but often individuals are good at something. The uneven cognitive profile of people with autism means great talent can be combined with striking disability in other areas.

Other behaviours resulting from autistic spectrum disorders may seem strange, and can result in problems for the individual and those around them.

Repetitiveness

This can take the form of repeating words or actions, and may be obsessive. For example, the individual may repeat words or sentences constantly, or ask the same question again and again. Or the individual may repeat the same actions or activity over and over, or always do things the same way, or go by the same route. These kinds of repetitive actions are often a response to anxiety. Doing or saying the same thing creates a calming sense of predictability. This can be positive for the individual. However, this repetitive behaviour can also take over and dominate someone's life. Individuals therefore need support to keep this behaviour at a reasonable level.

> *Tom's mum says:*
>
> Tom has always loved to have balls of string to thread through his fingers and we managed to negotiate this to be a private pleasure so they are kept in Tom's room. At times the string handling can become quite feverish in intensity.

Preoccupation

This can be a preoccupation with particular topics, objects, sets of things, or people, perhaps again to the point of obsession. It may be seen as the downside of characteristics such as single-mindedness and focus.

John says:

Knowing so much about football gives me lots to talk about to people who are interested in football, but I have real difficulty knowing when I should stop talking because people are fed up with me or they do not want to hear any more about football.

Resistance to change

As the National Autistic Society put it so neatly, *'Variety is not the spice of life.'* People with autism may resent, resist, and become very distressed at change or loss, especially if it is sudden. Major life events such as bereavement and moving house can be even more traumatic for them. But even a small change, such as taking a different-coloured taxi into town, may cause serious upset. When you have little ability to work out the consequences of changes or what the possible significance is of a different-coloured taxi it makes even these small changes very frightening.

Thinking point

Consider the last time someone with autism you support appeared anxious and distressed. Was this connected with some kind of change in routine or something being altered in their environment? Consider also how we can make changes that are less scary and more acceptable to the individual.

Problems with making choices

It can be difficult to adjust to the fact that for people who have autism, limiting choice may be more supportive.

As an example, a person with autism may be able to reel off the names of every breakfast cereal on the shelves of a supermarket they visited a week ago. But if left to choose from them all, the same person will do so only with difficulty, or not at all. It may be necessary to restrict choice to a selection of two or three.

> *Tom says:*
>
> I really want people to understand how difficult choice is for me and other people with autism. People may think they are being kind offering me lots of choices but they are not, lots of choice makes me feel very, very anxious.

Reaction to sensory experience

An individual who has autism may overreact or under react to sights, sounds, scents, touch and other sensations. Donna Williams, who has autism, has written about her different way of sensing things and the way in which people on the autistic spectrum may be sensitive or insensitive to certain stimuli. If we know about this in advance when we are supporting individuals it can help to prevent any increase in anxiety due to sensory overload.

> *Tom's mum says:*
>
> Fire bells or hand driers in public toilets need to be flagged up in advance and explained or they can be very frightening indeed for Tom.

Wanting to be alone

Many people with autism experience this. It may be a response to people or situations they find too much, or come from a wish to be left undisturbed with some preoccupation. It is not so much the need which is exceptional. Most people feel like this on occasion. But the length of time involved and the frequency of the urge to be alone may appear odd. We need to be aware of this tendency but also take care not to use it as an excuse to try to avoid engaging with an individual. People with autism need to learn the value of human relationships and it is our job to help them with this.

> *Tom says:*
>
> I find being with people very tiring and often need quite a lot of time on my own if I have been out to dinner with my circle of support. But I do enjoy my circle meetings.

Bizarre conduct

People who have autism may display any of a number of strange repetitive movements. These include rocking to and fro, jumping, twisting and turning, flicking fingers or objects in front of the eyes, and flapping hands.

> *John says:*
>
> Like many people with autism I like to flap but I tend to do it with a specific piece of card and in my pocket or where others can't see me. I have learnt this is more acceptable.

Activity

Think of an individual you support or have supported with autism. Write down all the behaviours they display which are part of their autism, such as flapping or wanting to be alone. Remember to include behaviours which can be seen as a strength, such as an ability to remember specific dates.

Causes of autistic spectrum conditions

What causes autism is still not known. Research is beginning to provide some indications. It is also helping to dispel some old myths. The following are no more than key aspects of present evidence-based thinking about possible causes:

- It is not clear whether there is a single cause or group of causes of autism.

- The origins of autism are now suspected to be organic, rather than psychological.

- It is now considered less likely that autism is due to physical damage to the brain before or during birth.

- Much of current research centres on the 'autistic brain' functioning differently, perhaps connected to problems with its development at or around the time of birth.

- There is a growing body of evidence to suggest that autism is a genetic condition. Studies of twins where one twin has autism have suggested there may be a genetic predisposition to autistic spectrum disorders and related conditions.

- In 2001, researchers working on information from the Human Genome Project found indications that certain genes may increase susceptibility to autism.

- Research is complicated by the possibility that autism is not a single condition which emerges in a spectrum of forms, but a range of developmental disorders of the brain.

At least two additional factors should always be kept in mind when considering these and other developments in identifying the causes of autism:

- Even if the causes are found to be genetic, we will still have to take into account the effect of an individual's environment interacting with his or her genetic predisposition.

- The social model of disability suggests people are not disabled by their impairments, but rather by environmental considerations such as the fact that society is arranged in ways which restrict or exclude them.

The myths

Autism has seized the public imagination. There remains a great deal of mystery about it. Not surprisingly from these circumstances a mythology has emerged. Some of these myths can be damaging or hurtful to people who have autism and their families. It is important to be equipped to distinguish myth from research and genuine debate.

- Autism is not a personality disorder, or mental illness, although like other people those with autism may develop such problems.

- There is no miracle cure for autism, either in medical science or complementary and alternative medicine, but there is a great deal that can be done to lessen the difficulties having autism can bring.

- Autism is not caused by parents raising their children in an emotionally distant way – the so-called 'cold parents' or 'refrigerator parents' – although parents have a major role to play in supporting children who have autism.

Ongoing debates

Why are cases of autism on the increase? One view is that awareness of autism is relatively new among parents and health professionals, and as a result children and adults are being diagnosed with autism that would have been overlooked in the past. But the number of cases found is increasing rapidly, and there are arguments that increased awareness does not account for this, and that other factors may be involved which require investigation.

An awareness of current research on autistic spectrum conditions makes an important contribution to the provision of good quality support for people with autism and their families. New information is emerging all the time and may well have become available since this book was published. The resources listed at the end of this chapter and the following chapters include contact details for a number of organisations, which you can use to keep yourself up to date. If you are a professional supporting people with autistic spectrum conditions you should try and keep up to date with the latest research in order to ensure the knowledge base underpinning your day-to-day practice is well informed. This will help maintain and improve the standard of support you and colleagues offer to people with autism and their families.

Key points from this chapter

- The spectrum of autism includes the uneven levels of ability that people have. Don't make assumptions about what people can or can't do.

- Always value the individuality of the person with autism that you know. Treat them with dignity and respect.

- When trying to understand someone with autistic spectrum conditions, look carefully at the four key areas outlined in this chapter.

  1. Communication.

  2. Social Interaction.

  3. Rigid ways of thinking.

  4. Sensory differences and difficulties.

- Person centred working means treating people with dignity, upholding their rights and respecting their individuality.

References and where to go for more information

References

Attwood, T (2007) *The Complete Guide to Asperger's Syndrome.* London: Jessica Kingsley Publishers

Good Autism Practice, a journal published twice a year by BILD. For more information go to www.bild.org.uk

Johnston, P and Hatton, S (2003) *Conversations in Autism – From Insight to Good Practice.* Kidderminster: BILD

Jordan, R (2001) *Autism with Severe Learning Difficulties.* London: Souvenir Press

Lawson, W (2003) *Build Your Own Life.* London: Jessica Kingsley Publishers

Tilly, L (2011) *Person Centred Approaches when Supporting People with a Learning Disability.* Exeter: Learning Matters/BILD

Websites

Autism Alliance www.autism-alliance.org.uk

Autism Cymru www.awares.org

National Autistic Society www.autism.org.uk

Scottish Autism www.scottishautism.org

Stephen Wiltshire – an artist with autism www.stephenwiltshire.co.uk

Chapter 2

Understanding the behaviours of some people with autistic spectrum conditions

Tom says:

It is very important to understand autism or you may think I am being rude or difficult when I don't mean to be. I don't find eye contact very easy but I am listening when you speak to me.

Tom and Alex chat at the Slug and Lettuce.

Introduction

If you are new to providing a service or support to a person with autism you may observe that their behaviour is different from non autistic people. You may find some of their behaviours difficult to understand and, as Tom commented above, you may wrongly think that the person is being rude or deliberately difficult. If you have an understanding of how the person's autism might affect their behaviour then you will be better prepared and able to provide good person centred support.

Behavioural characteristics associated with autistic spectrum conditions

The behaviours of people with autistic spectrum conditions can be unusual and you need to take care not to make assumptions about what they mean. The most likely thing is that you will be wrong because you will not be thinking in an autism friendly way.

A scenario

Mark, aged 14, is the eldest of three siblings and has a diagnosis of autism. Mark loves the story of Aladdin and watches the DVD over and over again. He also likes to look at a book he has of the story and to have it read to him. Mark's mum discovers that the pantomime at the local theatre before Christmas is going to be Aladdin and she points out the poster advertising it to Mark, who is very excited by it. Mark's mum discusses the idea of going to a performance with all three of the children once the schools have broken up for Christmas and the decision is made to attend. Angie, the sessional support worker who helps with Mark during the school holidays, agrees to come and support Mark's mum to attend with the three children at an afternoon performance. Mark can get agitated in crowds and this can sometimes lead to self-injury, but his mum makes detailed plans and feels they could cope.

When planning an outing or new activity, think about how the person with autism might react.

As they enter the theatre Mark is upset by the crowd of other children and families but with his favourite drink and the promise of his usual strawberry yoghurt at the interval he settles into his seat and when the actors come on stage he is enthralled.

The first time the lamp is rubbed for the genie to appear Mark jumps up in a panic and begins to pull his mum from her seat, saying 'Fire! Fire!' as the dry ice machine puffs out smoke and the genie appears. Mark is now screaming and dragging his mum towards the door, leaving his brother and sister upset and embarrassed. His love of Aladdin seems to have disappeared.

Mark wants to leave the building and is now in quite an anxious state. Staff at the theatre ask if they can help but then back away as Mark begins to bite his arm and hit his head. Angie comes out to support Mark's mum and, seeing the level of behaviour, suggests that they go home. His mum quickly agrees and Angie goes to get the younger two out of the theatre. They get into the car with Mark still biting his hand, and the younger children angry and upset. Once in the car Mark has his strawberry yoghurt and begins to calm down. Mark begins to tell the story of Aladdin while everyone else in the car remains angry, upset and frustrated. They go home in silence apart from Mark, who is happily repeating over and over, 'Genie, genie of the lamp'.

Understanding the behaviour

Let's begin by looking at all the things Mark's mum did right to plan for this trip and why what she did was right for someone with autistic spectrum conditions. She picked something that she knew Mark liked, as the story of Aladdin was one of his current special interests. She knew it was not just the DVD, as he liked the book as well and he had seen the posters advertising the pantomime and was excited by them.

Mark's mum knew the crowds might be a problem and was prepared with two things that were important to Mark: a particular kind of drink and strawberry yoghurt. She also had Angie the support worker with her who knew Mark. What Mark's mum had not been able to prepare for was that a dry ice machine would be used to produce smoke and this would lead to Mark thinking there was a fire. This then led to Mark becoming distressed and injuring himself. This made it necessary to leave the theatre as this was the only option available to get away from the source of Mark's anxiety and distress.

For most children, the smoke being made when the lamp was rubbed would have caused no anxiety; rather it would have caused excitement at the thought of seeing the genie. This is because most children would be able to quickly understand that this kind of smoke was safe. Mark had been taught that smoke means fire and fire is dangerous and you must get away. He was unable to think flexibly and see this kind of smoke in a different context. This is because of his autism. Mark became stressed and anxious because the people around him did not see things as he saw them. His stress and anxiety led to his self injury and a very stressful situation for everyone concerned.

Reasons why people with autistic spectrum conditions may exhibit certain behaviours

Let's think about the four key areas of autistic spectrum conditions, covered in Chapter 1, in relation to the above scenario and identify how these might help us in understanding the person's behaviour.

Language and communication

Mark was able to calm down with words of reassurance and the visual support of something special to him that he liked the taste of. The special drink his mum had taken helped Mark through his anxiety about the crowds of people in the theatre. However, his fear and anxiety at the sight of the smoke from the dry ice machine prevented him from being able to hear or understand anything else that was said. His ability to understand spoken words was severely affected by his level of anxiety.

It was very sensible of Angie not to get involved and start to try and talk to Mark, as lots more talking would have made him more agitated in this situation.

Social interaction

Mark was agitated by the crowds. He knew he was going to see the story of Aladdin and his mum had explained something of what it might be like but she had said nothing about other people being there. To most it would be obvious that other people would go to see a pantomime. However, Mark's autism means he is very unaware of what other people may or may not do. Social situations are difficult for him and he does not really understand why other people are around, but he was excited about the things that were important to him: Aladdin, the special drink and the strawberry yoghurt.

Ways of thinking and behaving

The fact that Mark's younger brother and sister were upset was also of no significance to Mark as he was hardly aware of them. This can make Mark appear to be very selfish and often people with autism are thought to be selfish. But Mark does not have the ability to think about others in the same way as non autistic people. His attention was very focused on the story of Aladdin until the smoke and then there was only one thing in his mind – to get away from the smoke. As this did not happen quickly he began to exhibit a behaviour that we all find stressful. Mark began to hurt himself. It got what he wanted, to get out of the building. So here again Mark appears to be very selfish.

In Chapter 1 we heard from Tom about how important predictability is and that when things happen in a predictable pattern he finds it calming. This can be true for something like self injury. Mark was starting a predictable pattern of self injury. It may be a negative predictable pattern but for the individual with autism it is the predictability that is most important. The self injury in this situation was a way of trying to control his anxiety. It blocked out the confusing situation that had developed and made things happen in the way he needed them to. The self injury stopped when he was finally calm, in the car, and eating strawberry yoghurt, with little regard to everyone else's feelings. This was not because Mark is selfish, rather because Mark is autistic.

Sensory experiences

The hustle and bustle of the crowds was difficult for Mark, but his mum knew that this would be the case and she did her best to keep him focused and have some useful distractions. The dry ice machine that made the smoke was a real sensory overload for Mark and one that he associated with fire and with fear. Once focused on the fear and with his anxiety levels very high there was little that could be done to bring his sensory experience of the situation back under control.

There is a lot more information about the reasons why people may show certain behaviours in a book by Sharon Paley in this series, *Promoting Positive Behaviour when Supporting People with a Learning Disability and People with Autism*.

Supporting people with autistic spectrum conditions when they are anxious or stressed

If you are supporting someone with an autistic spectrum condition there is quite a lot to think about. You need to get to know them and their autism. You need to consider what makes them anxious and how best you can avoid this or support them to cope with their anxiety, just as Mark's mum did. It won't always work and you also need to have your backup plans in case something like sensory overload happens or the person you support develops extreme feelings of anxiety.

- Understanding autism really helps you support people with autism more effectively.

- Be prepared for what might happen and think in an autism friendly way.

Activity

Think about someone you support with autistic spectrum conditions and what kind of behaviour they exhibit when they are anxious. What could you use that this person finds calming to reduce their anxiety and problematic behaviour when it occurs? Write your ideas down and discuss implementing them, with colleagues, other supporters or the individual themselves, if appropriate.

John says:

If I have a difficult day when things do not go according to plan and I arrive home agitated and anxious, the best thing for me to do is to go to my room and spend an hour or so reading my bus timetables. They are so lovely with the numbers and the times and the different routes they go on. They are so predictable and calming.

John enjoying a day out in Bath.

John's words show that he understands himself and his personal experience of the autistic spectrum. He has learnt that the bus timetables are calming because they are so predictable and he makes good use of this knowledge. His family have come to accept this as well so no one tries to persuade him to throw the timetables away anymore. It is less easy for those who are unable to have such a good grasp of themselves and their autism, although many people can learn to understand themselves and their behaviours to some degree.

Thinking point

Do you give a sense of value to the things that individuals with autism find special and important in their lives?

Do you sometimes forget to let an individual with autism know that a change is going to happen because for you the change is almost insignificant?

The challenges of having autism

Alex is another young man who has helped in the writing of this book. He has spent several years in a residential special school, which to begin with he found very challenging. He was extremely anxious most days and would shout and scream and sometimes hit and kick staff.

Alex says:

I was frightened of the other students as I did not know what they would do. I liked to control everything so I had lots and lots of rituals to help me keep control and to make life predictable so it was not so scary. I only washed once a week, I had to be last out of a room, I liked to eat outside and I needed to watch all my television programmes, **all of them**. I could not go out if there was any risk that I might not be back in time for my programmes.

I do still like things to be predictable but I have learnt that this is due to having autism. Learning about my own autism has made such a difference to my life.

It does make such a difference if an individual can learn to understand themselves and their autism. This should be an aim with anybody supporting an individual with autistic spectrum conditions, no matter what their level of ability or learning disability. Good support means always asking questions and considering why behaviour is happening. Considering behaviour and incidents through the four key areas of autism can help you to identify triggers. Thinking 'with an autistic hat on' is essential. So many people with autistic spectrum conditions do not understand themselves or their autism so you need to do the understanding for them. Examining behaviours from a perspective informed by a good knowledge of autism and the challenges it presents for an individual can result in solutions that can have a radically positive impact.

Elizabeth, mum to Edward who has autism and is non verbal, says:

When Edward is tired or hot or there is too much going on he will often sit down and refuse to move. We have had some very difficult times when this has happened. However, if we can watch carefully and ensure we stop talking and just show Edward a picture of one of his favourite things like pizza or ice-cream, then he will keep walking a little longer. Next we have to make sure we can produce the pizza or the ice-cream! The secret is to be one step ahead all the time and mostly we are, but there are times when everything goes wrong and then Edward is not the only one who gets upset, I do as well because I feel I have let him down. Autism can be very hard work for both of us.

People with autism often feel out of control and this is very frightening for them. It is the fear and anxiety that they experience so frequently that leads to behaviour that is challenging for you and of course for them. Often it is as if they are left with nothing else they can do except scream and shout and hit out in the hope that somehow the world will start to make sense again. Often behaviours like kicking and lashing out lead to something predictable and calming, even if that is being restrained. Or it could be that the physical repetitive action of biting or kicking is in itself providing a predictability, albeit a painful type of predictable feeling. Negative predictable patterns are very common for people with autism. The challenge is to try to give predictability in a positive and appropriate way. This can often be very hard to achieve.

Neil, a manager of a home for people with autism, describes a difficulty he is having with Paul, one of the men living at the home:

Things have changed here recently with new staff and the redecoration and Paul has become very anxious. He keeps pulling staff towards him and down on to the ground so they are on top of him. Once they are on the floor with him he calms down. It is as if he likes having a member of staff on top of him. But of course staff cannot stay in this position and they get up in order to get away and avoid being grabbed. This seems to make Paul more agitated and he starts jumping up and going to grab another member of staff to pull to the floor.

Activity

Read the example above again and then answer the questions below. Discuss your ideas with a colleague or your line manager.
- *Why do you think Paul was doing this to staff?*
- *Which area of autism would you most associate the behaviour with?*
  1. *Language and communication?*
  2. *Social interaction?*
  3. *Ways of thinking and behaving?*
  4. *Sensory issues?*
- *What could be done differently to help Paul to be calmer?*

Trying to work out what this behaviour is about is the challenge for staff, and it's a situation where you need to do a bit of detective work really. You need to ask what Paul is saying by this behaviour. What could he be trying to communicate, and also what is he getting from having staff on top of him? What is the benefit for him? If you can work this out you might be able to address his needs in a more appropriate way. But you have to try and work out what the behaviour is about first.

Tom's mum says:

Living with autism can be hard work but there are times when I am grateful for Tom's attention to detail and ability to focus. Last year on return from holiday we had been delayed at the airport and when we finally landed back in the UK it was late and we were all tired. Suddenly we began to panic about which car park we had left the car in and where we had to catch the bus to the car park. It was with much relief and gratitude that we just followed Tom to the right bus stop, Car Park C and the exact position of our car. A detail like that would not have escaped Tom because for him this kind of thing is very important and delayed aeroplanes or tiredness do not alter that.

Tom says:

There are things I am very good at. I remember things that others forget, like what we had to eat for my birthday last year, what date we visited York and always where we park the car. I can be very useful.

Autism friendly ways of supporting people

There are lots of ways you can help support people with autism. We carried out a small survey when we were putting this book together. Forty people who are expert professionals in the field of autism or people who themselves have an autistic spectrum condition were asked what they felt were the five most important things to do when working with someone with autistic spectrum conditions. The replies were remarkably similar from all of our respondents.

The top five replies were:

1. Keep a calm atmosphere.

2. Keep the environment calm and uncluttered (unless it is objects that the individual really wants around them).

3. Get a good structure to the day – individuals do not have to be busy all the time but they do need to know what is happening.

4. Give visual support to those who need help to understand the structure of the day – this will include some people who are very able as well as those with a learning disability.

5. Work at getting to know individuals with autism and engage with them through the things that are of significance and importance to them.

Key points from this chapter

- Behaviours that you may find challenging happen for a reason. It may be difficult to find the reason but one thing that helps is if you can try and think in an autistic way and remember the all-important need for predictability.

- Always remember that if you can understand the autism you will make much more sense of the behaviour.

- Once you have unravelled the autism behind the behaviour you will be better equipped to know what to do and also how to prevent challenges next time.

- Autism can bring gifts and skills. Always try and consider how to make good use of them and value what the individuals can do as well as what they find challenging.

References and where to go for more information

References

Alex with Hatton, S (2005) 'The more we learn – the better we understand: Alex's story', *Good Autism Practice*, May 2005

Clements, J (2005) *People with Autism Behaving Bad.* London: Jessica Kingsley Publishers

National Autistic Society (2008) *Being Me – a self development resource pack from people on the autism spectrum* (DVD). London: NAS

Paley, S (2011) *Promoting Positive Behaviour when Supporting People with a Learning Disability and People with Autism.* Exeter: Learning Matters and BILD

Welton, J (2008) *Can I tell you about my Asperger Syndrome? A Guide for Friends and Family.* London: Jessica Kingsley Publishers

Websites

Autism Alliance www.autism-alliance.org.uk

Autism Cymru www.awares.org

National Autistic Society www.autism.org.uk

Scottish Autism www.scottishautism.org

Chapter 3

Communicating effectively with a person with autistic spectrum conditions

It means a lot to Tom to know exactly what is happening and to be able to **SEE** it. Sue's timetables are very autism friendly and too often people do not understand Tom's level of need for predictability. Tom's ability to talk and read and travel independently masks his deep need for more visual communication.

Tom's mum

Tom and Sue.

Introduction

A person with autistic spectrum conditions is very likely to have a difficulty with communication and this is often not understood well enough by those supporting them. It may be, as with Tom above, that people assume a greater level of understanding than there is. Alternatively, someone who is non-verbal and is thought to understand very little may actually listen to what others say and may be ready at the door waiting to go home for the weekend when no one has specifically helped them to understand that they are going home. This is the kind of thing that can baffle people.

We all need to learn that we should never assume a level of ability based on the fact that someone with autism either speaks a great deal or does not speak at all. Rather we need to get to know the person and how their autism has impacted on them.

Learning outcomes

This chapter will help you to:

- explain why it is important to be aware of the impact of your own verbal and non-verbal communication on an individual with an autistic spectrum condition;

- identify aspects of the environment that affect communication with an individual;

- describe how to reduce barriers to communication with an individual;

- outline the use of visual communication systems for individuals who have an autistic spectrum condition;

- identify who could provide advice about effective communication with an individual.

This chapter covers:

Level 2 LD 210 – Introductory awareness of autistic spectrum conditions: Learning Outcome 5

The impact of your verbal and non-verbal communication on an individual with autism

'Autism friendly' communication is the key to providing good support. In order to know what autism friendly communication is we need first of all to explore the difficulties people with autism have with communication.

A scenario

Tazneem (known to everyone as Taz), a woman with Asperger syndrome, goes into a department store to buy a jumper. She finds the jumper she wants and then goes to what she thinks is the correct place to pay for the jumper. At the desk there is a woman on the phone and Taz appears not to realise she is on the phone as she takes £20 from her purse and hands it to the woman. The woman draws back her hand, dropping the £20 note. She covers the receiver of the phone and says to Taz, 'This is not the till; you pay over there near to the escalator.' The woman then resumes her phone conversation.

Taz stares at her and after a few seconds tries again to put the £20 in her hand and shows her the jumper she is trying to pay for. Exasperated, the woman repeats herself only this time she says,'Look, this is not where you pay, the tills are over by the escalator, and you can pay there, not here, OK?'

Taz walks off baffled and muttering, 'Well I will take it home then and not bother paying if you don't want my money'.

As she gets close to the escalator she finds she is thinking about the word escalator and the phrase that she had not really grasped before, 'tills by the escalator'. She looks up and sees someone giving money to a woman behind a till. 'Oh!', thinks Taz, 'I must have been in the wrong place. "Tills by the escalator", that's what the woman meant. She could have explained it to me properly.'

Communication is not just about speaking, it is about understanding

Taz has Asperger syndrome and so there were a number of difficulties for her in the situation described above. Taz is very focused on what she is doing herself and does not easily notice that someone might have their attention elsewhere. She did not notice that the woman she tried to give the money to was on the phone and she did not notice that there was no till on the information desk where the woman was sitting. Taz also did not notice the sign saying information desk. Donna Williams, you may recall from a previous chapter, calls this being mono channelled. Like Taz, Donna is often thought to be selfish and unaware of other people and their needs, but like Taz she has an autistic spectrum condition and this actually makes it very difficult for her to be aware of others.

The woman did explain to Taz where to go and pay, and here we have a good example of the processing delay that people with autistic spectrum conditions have, especially when they are not expecting to hear the words that come at them. Taz could not grasp what was being said, she stared as she tried to process the words and work out why what she expected to happen (that her money would be taken and her new jumper put into a bag for her to take home) was not happening.

Taz says these kinds of things happen to her all the time and she is aware now, as an older woman with an autistic spectrum condition, that people often think she is either deaf or stupid. Taz is actually a highly intelligent woman but she has autism and all the communication difficulties that go with that:

- a processing delay;

- poor ability to read non-verbal language;

- lack of awareness of the situation other people are in that would give a clue to the communication.

At the other end of the autism spectrum, David, a man with severe learning disabilities and an autistic spectrum condition, may have learnt to repeat the last option given to him when asked a question. This is called echolalia. David seems to be very capable and to easily understand what is being said to him. When David is offered a choice by the staff at the day service he attends, he seems able to make a clear decision, such as choosing a tuna sandwich over a cheese one. However, his echolalia is easily identified by giving him a nonsense choice last. For example, when David is asked, 'Would you like a cheese or jellyfish sandwich?', his surprising reply is 'jellyfish'. David has learnt that repeating the last thing he hears quickly will get the person to stop asking him things he does not understand and leave him alone, to fiddle with his string or complete his favourite puzzle. This sometimes means of course that David ends up with sandwiches, or activities or a host of other things, which he does not in fact want. This can then lead to challenging behaviour and staff at the day service struggling to cope when David throws his lunch on the floor or starts hitting himself when they ask him to get out of the minibus.

What is clear from the two examples above is that people with autistic spectrum conditions can have some real difficulties with communication and even when people speak to us, and in the case of Taz are extremely articulate, they still have a communication problem. This is difficult for us to remember, but it is important to do so if we are going to support people well.

Activity

Think of the last time you felt someone with an autistic spectrum condition was being difficult or awkward or even deliberately ignoring you. Did they really understand your communication? What do you think? Go over the incident in your mind or talk to a colleague about it. You may begin to realise the communication difficulties in autism are often not easy to see at first.

Reducing the barriers to communication with an individual with autism

There are several things you can do to communicate in a more autism friendly way that will help to reduce the barriers to communication for the person you work with. Always bear in mind the different ways in which people with autistic spectrum conditions think and process information. Make your verbal communication as slow, clear and real as possible. Avoid metaphors, or other figures of speech, as people with autism might take them literally. For example, comments such as, 'Sonya is a real pig when she eats' or, 'My head was spinning with new ideas' might be disturbing for a person who takes them literally. Try to be predictable in your responses. Often people with autistic spectrum conditions will enjoy communicating with you in a set way initially, with specific greetings to which they will enjoy the same replies. This is a great way of building a relationship with the individual and although you may find it tiresome to always be asked the same question when you see them, try to remember the predictability of your response makes the individual feel calm and at ease.

Give the individual you are communicating with plenty of processing time. You may be surprised by how much time is needed; however, have patience and do not pressurise them for a response. Expect the pace of communication to be slower and allow for the person with autistic spectrum conditions to digest what you are saying to them and think about a response in their own time. This simple slowing down can have a dramatic impact. Also, try using much shorter sentences with emphasis on key words. Obviously this is particularly important when communicating with individuals with a learning disability and autistic spectrum conditions; however, people with Asperger syndrome or high functioning autistic spectrum conditions may also find more processing time helpful.

No matter where the person with autistic spectrum conditions falls on the autism spectrum, communication should always be made as concrete and predictable as possible. People with autistic spectrum conditions find it hard to work out the future and what other people might be thinking. They can become highly anxious if they don't understand what is about to happen, or what you are trying to communicate, and this anxiety can lead to harmful or dangerous behaviour. Good communication is therefore central to reducing anxiety for the individual with autistic spectrum conditions. It is the key way in which we can help people with autism function in what can be for them a confusing and terrifying world. Our aim when we are communicating should be to reduce anxiety, increase predictability and develop the individual's ability to function happily in the neurotypical world.

Using visual communication systems for a person with an autistic spectrum condition

There are many effective practical ways you can support an individual with autism friendly communication. We need to understand the very concrete and visual way that people with autistic spectrum conditions think. Temple Grandin, who has autistic spectrum conditions, calls it 'thinking in pictures' and uses this as the title for one of her books. The problem with our spoken words is that they are gone so quickly. A picture is much more concrete and lasting. Written words, like a picture, can be looked at over and over again, and they can be carried around, so they often bring reassurance.

Tom, the co-writer of this book, comes to stay with me sometimes and when he comes we do very similar things. However, what he likes to see when he arrives is his timetable for the weekend. I ensure there is a copy in his room for him to carry around and also a copy is pinned up in the kitchen.

> *Tom says:*
>
> I like to have my timetable when I stay at Sue's, I read it and think about the definite things that will happen. Having a predictable plan typed out for me is calming and enjoyable.

Photos, pictures and symbols make what is going to happen next very real for somebody with autistic spectrum conditions. Sequences of photographs or pictures arranged on a daily or weekly basis, preferably put in place by the individual using the timetable themselves, can be an amazingly effective support. This communication support combats the individual's inability to predict the future and makes daily events less terrifying.

The individual using the timetable can look at the timetable as many times as they wish and this can also reduce repetitive questioning. However, too often visual timetables are constructed and then neglected or left to get out of date. They can easily be criticised as ineffective if not created and maintained with care. They in fact require a huge amount of effort and investment if they are to remain an effective support. It is unsurprising that if the events displayed on the timetable do not happen, or they happen in a different sequence during this time, that the individual using the timetable either gets upset or stops taking notice of what can become a lie. Photos and pictures must be kept up to date and changed to reflect any change in activities. An example of one of Tom's timetables is shown below:

Tom's stay at Sue and Peter's

	Morning	Afternoon	Evening
Friday		Dad will drive Tom to Sue's and will arrive at about 5pm.	Tom to have time to himself. Sue to cook the evening meal and we will eat at 7.30. Tom will help clear away and then have time to himself.
Saturday	Sue will walk the dog and then breakfast at 9am. Sue and Tom will leave at 11am for the shops in Bristol. Tom will have time to himself but we will have lunch together at 1pm. Tom to choose the place for lunch.	We will come back from Bristol at about 3pm. Sue will take the dog out and Tom is welcome to join her or have time to himself. Tom will cook the evening meal of spaghetti bolognese.	Tom will serve the evening meal of spaghetti bolognese. We will eat about 7pm. Sue and Peter will wash up. Tom to have time to himself.
Sunday	Sue will walk the dog. Breakfast at 9am. Sue and Peter will be at church in the morning and Tom is welcome to come and then have time to himself. Sue will cook lunch for 1pm.	After lunch Sue and Peter will walk the dog out by the river and Tom is welcome to join them. At 4pm we have been invited to Sue's friend Carmel's house for tea and cake if Tom would like to come.	In the evening Tom can get himself a sandwich and have time to himself.
Monday	Sue will walk the dog and breakfast will be at 8.30am. Tom can have his final walk around the area and be ready to leave for home at 11am. **Sue will take Tom home in time for lunch.**		

A good visual timetable, using photos and symbols, can be useful for many people. If it uses photos specific to the individual, which are instantly recognisable to them, this can be particularly helpful. However, the timetable needs to be maintained in order to remain effective. So, for example, if a different member of staff is going to be helping, or a visit is going to involve a different local shop, the photos need to change. An inaccurate visual timetable is worse than no timetable at all, as it means the person using the timetable cannot trust it to help them predict what is about to happen. Once they doubt the timetable, it is no longer capable of reducing their anxiety. For people at the other end of the spectrum, such as for Tom as referred to earlier, a calendar or diary with events written down can be more appropriate. The idea, however, is exactly the same; their anxiety is eased by making sure what will take place in the future is more concrete.

Using the method of sequencing adopted in a timetable can also be used to support choice making. Giving the individual two different photographs of the options available, and allowing plenty of time to process the choices on offer, can prove extremely helpful. The photographs make the choices less abstract and back up the words spoken.

Similar visual sequencing can also be a way of introducing a new idea or new experience, especially if you can show visually that the new activity will be immediately followed by the familiar and the predictable.

A good way of vocalising this alongside the visual aid is by using 'first' and 'then':

This may be helpful for someone who does not like doing the cleaning but loves going out to eat, and especially eating the food in the photograph. It helps them to see they will get to do what they want and very soon.

> *Elizabeth, mum to Edward who has autism and is non-verbal, says:*
>
> As long as we have the photos of things that Edward likes to show him, so that he knows we will soon be home or the car is not very far away, he will calm down. Edward can understand the words but they don't help. The photos do. Using photos to support communication with Edward is essential.

Tom likes to have written labels in his bedroom to help him organise his things and to enable him to be more independent.

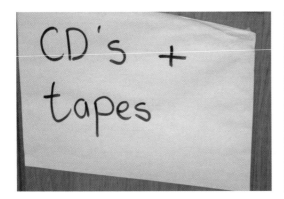 

For some individuals, a photo may not be meaningful. This is when it is good to try using an 'object of reference', that is, if you are asking the person to clean first and then go to the shop you may need to show them a cleaning cloth and then the bag they like to take to the shop.

Activity

1. *Think of someone you support who may benefit from the use of some photos to assist their understanding. Remember even if you feel sure they understand many of your spoken words, backing what you say up with photos can really help.*

2. *Start small. Use photographs, pictures or objects of reference to support the individual to make a choice about an activity or to show them what is happening next.*

3. *Ask yourself (and discuss with a colleague or friend if appropriate), is the use of visual aids improving our communication? If it is, think about expanding your use of visual support to a simple timetable. Remember how important it is to maintain this, keeping photos up to date and in sequence. It is vital the person with autistic spectrum conditions can trust the support you are putting in place.*

There are different visual ways to support communication. For some people a photo may be too abstract and you will need to use an actual object to support the spoken word, such as showing a cup when asking if they want a drink, but do try with photographs. A digital camera is one of the most autism friendly tools you can use. Most importantly, however, when you communicate with somebody with autistic spectrum conditions it must suit them and be personal to them.

Thinking point

If you could not predict what might happen next, what a terrifying place the world would seem. By trying to understand autism and by communicating in an autism friendly way you have the power to reduce the feelings of terror many people with autistic spectrum conditions face on a daily basis.

Information and advice about effective communication with an individual

Often the best people to seek advice from are family members, so do make sure you listen carefully to the parents or siblings of the person you support. Don't think just because the person you support is an adult their mum or dad may not have much that is relevant to share with you – they will – so do ask for their help and advice around effective communication with their son or daughter. In addition, it would be good to get an up to date communication assessment from a speech and language therapist. Even if the person you support talks a great deal an assessment would indicate their level of understanding and their ability to process information.

Key points from this chapter

Our ability to communicate with those we seek to support is central to our work and these are some top tips to remember when you are supporting those with autism:

- Keep your language clear and concise.
- Use visual supports to aid communication.

- Give people time to process the communication.

- Communicate in an environment that the person finds calm and when they are relaxed.

References and where to go for more information

References

Grandin, T (2006) *Thinking in Pictures.* London: Bloomsbury Publishing

Bogdashina, O (2004) *Communication Issues in Autism and Asperger's syndrome.* London: Jessica Kingsley Publishers

Cohen, M and Sloan, L (2005) *Visual Supports for People with Autism.* Bethesda, MD: Woodbine House Inc.

Websites

Autism Alliance www.autism-alliance.org.uk

Autism Cymru www.awares.org

National Autistic Society www.autism.org.uk

Scottish Autism www.scottishautism.org

Chapter 4

Person centred support for people with autistic spectrum conditions

I have a circle of support and I really like to see my friends. We go to the pub and I talk about the Archers with Anne and the lovely city of York with Sue. I love it if there is custard to have with my pudding but I also really like to be on my own again and go for a walk without anyone else around. Having friends is important, I have learnt that, but they also have had to learn that I need time on my own.

Tom

Introduction

Working in a person centred way is quite simply getting to know the person so you are aware of their likes and dislikes, their strengths and needs, so you can support them in ways that work for them. This way of working helps the person to develop and take on new activities and challenges they may want to explore.

However, for someone with autistic spectrum conditions this needs to be done in an autism friendly way so as well as getting to know the individual you need to get to know their autistic spectrum condition and the impact it has on their life. It is only from a position of being really autism aware that you will be able to work in a person centred way with an individual with an autistic spectrum condition.

Learning outcomes

This chapter will help you to:

- understand why it is important to have in place structures and routines which match the wishes and needs of the individual;

- identify formal and informal support networks for an individual with an autistic spectrum condition;

- understand why it is important to involve families, friends and other paid carers in a person centred approach to the support of individuals with an autistic spectrum condition;

- develop ways of ensuring that the support provided is consistent, both within your own approach and with that of others;

- contribute towards the learning of an individual with an autistic spectrum condition.

This chapter covers:

Level 2 LD 210 – Introductory awareness of autistic spectrum conditions: Learning Outcome 4

Structures and routines which match the wishes and needs of the individual

John, a person with autism, says:

Autism for me is the quest for predictability.

A scenario

Joe has recently moved to a residential care home that is closer to where his parents live and to where he grew up. Joe seemed happy to move as long as he was able to do the two things that are very important to him: buying a can of cola from a nearby shop and getting a drink of cola at a nearby café. On being asked about how Joe was settling in the support worker said:

'We have been trying to do a person centred plan with Joe since he came to live here but there is so little he wants to do it is proving very difficult. He loves cola and enjoys going to the shop nearby to get a can or to the local café for a drink, but other than that we have found Joe very difficult to motivate – let alone get him to dream or get excited about doing something new and different in the future. In fact, staff are not very keen on trying to suggest too much to Joe as he can get quite agitated. We have had situations where Joe has been screaming and pushing staff out of the door and his screaming and shouting has gone on for a long time. We wonder if he is best left alone a lot of the time. People with autism do tend to like to be alone, don't they?'

One of the central values in health and social care is being person centred in the way that you work. This means having a good understanding of the needs and wishes of the person you support, treating them with dignity and respect and providing care in such a way as to promote their independence and choices. For many people with autism this will include having in place structures and routines that both provide predictability for the person, but that also allow them to grow and develop as an individual.

Valuing People Now (2009) is the government strategy that guides how people with learning disabilities are supported in England. Some people with learning disabilities also have autism as well. *Valuing People Now* has four guiding principles: rights, independent living, control and inclusion. It says that 'people should be involved in and in control of decisions made about their life. This is not usually doing exactly what you want, but it is about having information and support to understand the different options and their implications and consequences, so people can make informed decisions about their own lives'. One way of supporting people to achieve more choice and control is for people to create their own person centred plan. You may well have come across person centred plans in the work you do to support people already.

Typically a person centred plan identifies a person's strengths and needs, their likes and dislikes as well as their future goals. A plan often also describes the ways to support the individual to achieve the goals they have identified.

There are a number of different government policies and strategies that inform how people with autism should be supported by mainstream services such as in health and employment as well as by specialist services, for example of social care. These include *Fulfilling and Rewarding Lives: The Strategy for Adults with Autism in England*, and *The Autistic Spectrum Disorder (ASD) Strategic Action Plan for Wales*. For more information on these and other policies the book in this series *Next Steps in Supporting People with Autistic Spectrum Conditions* by Sue Hatton and John Simpson will help you.

In our opening scenario you can see how this can be less straightforward for people with autism. Joe's goals and desires, buying a can of cola, may seem very strange. Joe's autism also means he finds choice and the future particularly difficult concepts. Joe needs routine and sameness to create the predictability in his life which keeps him calm. Planning lots of changes is going to be very difficult for Joe, because he just wants things to stay the same.

So do we just leave Joe in his room with his can of cola and say that it is just his autism? Or do we try to understand why Joe is so fixated on cola and ask if he is really getting the most out of life? The challenge is to try and work with Joe in a person centred way and get an effective and meaningful person centred plan which accommodates his autism and yet helps him to develop and lead a rich and meaningful life. This is no easy task! Although a good knowledge of autism can help, creating an 'autism friendly' person centred plan will be very different for each individual.

John says:

New experiences can be very anxiety making so if I am going to do something new it is great to travel on a bus first. I love buses and find them calming so they are a way of helping me to try new things. Some people think it is strange that I would rather go by bus than get a lift, but they do not understand how the predictable routine of a bus journey is what gives me the courage to face a new experience that I **might** enjoy once I have got used to it.

John's words show us how important it is to get to know the person with autism you are supporting. You need to first understand the things they do enjoy and like, no matter how strange. These things, whether they are travelling by bus or buying a can of cola, can then be used to motivate them. This may mean buying a can of cola becomes the central feature of Joe's person centred plan, which at first may seem very strange indeed! However, this activity, which keeps Joe in our scenario calm and happy, can then be used to enrich and expand Joe's life in new directions. You will need to get to know the person you are working with well and try to understand their likes

Doing something predictable first, like catching a bus, can help a person before trying a new experience.

and dislikes 'with an autistic hat on'. If a drink of cola is the main motivator then use that as a starting point. You will need to invest a huge amount of time in helping a person with autism to develop and try new things. Again everything will depend on the individual, but the underlying need for predictability which affects everyone with autism will mean new things will be difficult. Don't give up on supporting the individual in a person centred way, it is just as important for someone with autism to develop and have new life experiences as it is for anyone. But creating a person centred plan for someone with autism will require you to really get to grips with their autism, and then to think creatively and carefully about how you can help them to progress.

Communication and being person centred

As discussed in the previous chapter, people with autistic spectrum conditions tend to be very visual thinkers and using pictures and writing things down helps to make our communication more concrete and real.

> *John says:*
>
> If life could be more like a bus timetable I would cope so much better – things happening at set times, all written out – but it isn't like that so much of the time and it is hard for people like me. It is great when those who work with me make the effort to give me more predictability by being definite. I prefer this to choices being offered though people find this hard to understand.

Social interaction and being person centred

Some people with autistic spectrum conditions are like Joe and may appear to want to be alone for much of the time. Many people are very happy in their own company. However, there is a danger that if a person spends too much time alone their mental health and wellbeing will deteriorate. For people like Joe we need to work hard at helping them to see and experience the value of human interaction. Of course we need to respect their need for time alone; however, this must not become unhealthy for the individual in question. If we offer the right kind of social interaction to the individual they should find pleasure in it and respond positively.

Again, remembering that autism affects people in hugely different ways is important. There are some individuals who are socially quite different and appear to want to be with people all the time. They may find it difficult to be on their own. Of course understanding 'their autism' may explain their behaviour.

> *Alex says:*
>
> I need to have staff around if I am not doing something specific or I get bored and lonely and then bad thoughts can come into my head. I am on my own at night now and sometimes I think people are going to break into the house or that the electrics won't work and I won't be able to make a cup of coffee. I can get very anxious when there is no one else around. I like to ask questions a lot and get the same answers. This helps me to feel calm.

Therefore to work with Alex in a person centred way you have to support him to be able to occupy himself when he is on his own. You also have to learn that when Alex asks lots of questions (ones that he knows the answers to already), you do need to give him a predictable response. Alex isn't trying to be funny or to annoy staff – without the same answers each time he is unable to remain calm. Alex calls these his 'anxiety questions' and as long as they are answered in the expected way Alex can cope with new experiences, or new suggestions being put to him.

Once you know whether the individuals you are supporting seek out company or seek to be alone, and you have found ways of engaging with each person that is predictable and based on the special interests that motivate them, you can begin to look at their relationships circles.

Identifying formal and informal support networks for an individual with an autistic spectrum condition

Relationships and friendships are important for people with an autistic spectrum condition even if they work in different ways. It can be important to support a visual understanding of how relationships work and one way to do this is to produce something that shows how people move in and out of your relationships circles as you get to know them or as staff change and move away.

Relationships circles

Relationships circles are a visual way to help someone understand who is in their life, how people come and go from their life and how to develop relationships to enhance the quality of their life in their own person centred way.

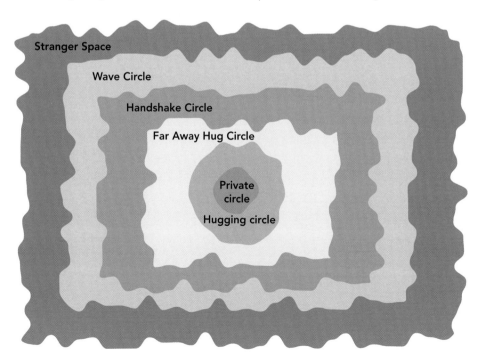

You would need to try and use language that means something to the individual. In this example I have used 'private circle', in which I would put a photo of the person whose relationship circle this is. Then comes the hugging circle, for close family and friends. Next is the far away hug, which is for people you do know and hug, but perhaps do not see that often. The handshake circle is next and then the wave circle and then the stranger space. This can be done with actual photos of people or written names. The idea is to include as many as possible of the people the person knows and also to show how people move, for example from the stranger space to the wave circle. To physically see how relationships develop and change helps the understanding of what relationships are. It helps the person to see more formal relationships, say with a doctor, social worker or employer, as well as the role that various support staff may play and what it means to be a friend or a person who is friendly.

This can be an enjoyable activity for the person you support to take part in as well as an educational one. The chart could go up on their bedroom wall and be a talking point to continue to go over how relationships work.

Thinking point

Does being person centred in the way you work mean that you become the friend of the individuals you support? Do you think it is possible to be a friendly member of staff but not a friend?

Activity

If it is appropriate, try producing a circle of relationships picture for someone with autism that you support and see if this helps them to understand who is in their life, and perhaps who they could see more of if they wanted to.

Involving family, friends and others in person centred support for a person with an autistic spectrum condition

Lucy is mum to Carl. Carl has autism and learning difficulties and he can be very challenging at times.

Lucy says:

Singing nursery rhymes is the best way to get to know my son; staff at the home he lives at have had to learn this, despite being worried that it seemed rather childish. Carl loves nursery rhymes, he always has. He does enjoy other kinds of music but when he gets anxious in a new place or with new people his favourite nursery rhymes are the best Carl friendly way to work with Carl.

If being 'person centred' is being 'Carl centred' then it is important that anyone working with Carl knows that one of the most predictable things in his life is the nursery rhymes that his family and those who work with Carl have been sharing with him and enjoying with him for many years.

It is also great if Carl's taste in music can grow and develop. Note that his mum does say he enjoys other music. So when Carl is calm and happy it would be good to introduce him to other music or varied versions of the nursery rhymes he loves so much.

Two of the most important sources of information about a person you support are parents and family.

To try and introduce change and new things to people with autistic spectrum conditions in order to give them the wider experience and perhaps learn about choice can only effectively be done from a position of calmness and contentment in the predictable world that helps them to feel safe.

Remember Joe's support worker from our scenario that started this chapter? She had tried to introduce new activities and ideas, but came to the conclusion Joe just liked his drink of cola and to be left alone.

But Joe's mum says:

Joe has always liked his drinks of cola. He also likes pictures of cola bottles and cans and photos of different members of the family drinking cola themselves. We used to have an album with photos of each of us drinking from a can or a bottle of cola. Joe would laugh and point to each of us and the cola. Joe also went horse riding at the local riding for the disabled club and he enjoyed swimming, but not in the public pool – just too many people around. We found a well off family near us who have their own pool and they let us use it twice a week when Joe was at home. Joe spent much of the time on the bottom of the pool as he seemed to like the feel of being underwater – he does this in the bath as well. Of course he always had to have a drink of cola after going riding or swimming but he did enjoy both activities.

In order to get to know someone who does not talk very well and is not able to tell us about themselves we have to become good investigators. One of the most important sources of information is parents and family. Joe's mum reveals so much and gives us many things to work with. Notice how important the drink of cola is. It is the motivator for Joe, however it has been used by his family brilliantly – to engage with Joe and make him laugh, to get Joe out and doing physical activities like swimming. The drink of cola is the predictable and much loved factor in Joe's life but it has been cleverly used to support Joe to explore new experiences and make these experiences feel safe.

When developing a person centred plan with an individual, their family and friends are an invaluable resource and can often be neglected or ignored. As support staff you need to work together with the family. Sometimes they may appear over-protective or disinterested, but try to remember their journey of life which will not have been easy. Get alongside them and listen carefully. You will learn valuable information to help you support the person with autism.

People with autistic spectrum conditions are inflexible thinkers and they do find change difficult and scary, but if we work in a very person centred and 'autism friendly' way then all sorts of things are possible.

Ensuring that support is consistent

Listening to family members is really important for making sure our approach to an individual with autism is consistent, and this also applies to mainstream services who might provide occasional support to a person, for example the dentist or GP. This is why person centred plans need to be living documents that lots of people get involved with, so that everyone involved in that individual's life knows the best way to work with them. It may be that there are disagreements between support staff or between staff and family members. These need to be talked about and an agreement reached so that there is a consistent approach to the person's support. While you are busy making sure everyone is involved please don't forget the person with autism and remember how often they can surprise us!

> *Tom says:*
>
> I may be 30 years old now but I still love custard and it is the thing I look for on a menu if we go out. But with help and support I have learnt to eat all sorts of food and in different kinds of places. I can even cope if there is no custard on the menu now, but it makes me feel sad. Once in the pub they said they had run out of syrup sponge pudding and people thought I would be upset but they still had the custard so I did not really care about the sponge pudding.

Thinking point

What are the predictable routines that someone you support enjoys? Think about how you and others help to maintain these routines with the person. Why might it be important for that person that their routines stay the same?

Activity

Try to think of a way of using something that is loved and predictable for an individual you support to extend their experiences in some way. Talk through your ideas with people who know the person well or, if it is appropriate, with the person.

Sensory issues and being person centred

Keeping in mind the sensory differences and difficulties that each individual with an autistic spectrum condition may have is important when you are working with them. It is also important to be aware that these can change. Someone who is usually noise sensitive may love one or two particular noises that surprise you. They may also enjoy an experience like a very fast roller coaster that you would not expect them to like. This is why it is important to have an understanding of the sensory experience for the person you support if you are going to be able to work in that all important person centred way.

Neurotypical people love to celebrate Christmas, Eid, birthdays and other special occasions. The decorations go up, the food can change, the shops are busier and even the things we talk about can be different. So it is not surprising that many people with autistic spectrum conditions find Christmas or Eid and other celebrations difficult. Think about this from a sensory point of view. We may notice the shops are busier, but do we then consider the impact of the extra noise and hustle and bustle for the person we support both in the home environment and in the community?

Tom says:

I like Christmas when it happens and the things we do in my family but I hate the busy shops and all the decorations, I find it really difficult that things are not in their usual place in the supermarket and all the different lights that flash and music everywhere, the build up to Christmas can be a very difficult time for me.

John says:

For me it is all the people, I get stressed in certain circumstances with lots of people around and when I am stressed I am not so able to know where my body is. It means I crash in to door frames and trolleys and people. I need to be able to shop when there are less people around, and not more, in order to be able to cope.

We learnt a bit about the sensory issues for people with autistic spectrum conditions in Chapter 1, and so to be able to work in a person centred way it is going to be important to have a real understanding of what those sensory issues are for the individual you work with. Remember to take account of all seven senses: hearing, seeing, taste, smell, touch, sense of balance and the sense of knowing where you are in space (your vestibular and proprioception senses).

Thinking point

- *What happens to you when you get stressed?*
- *Do you find that you have to turn the radio off in order to be able to concentrate?*
- *Do you find yourself tapping your foot or needing to chew gum on occasions?*
- *Our senses are affected by stress as well.*

Activity

Write out the names of the seven senses with the name of someone you support in the middle of a piece of paper. Write down one thing that you have noticed about their sensory experience in this area then talk about your findings with a colleague. Use your ideas to help you work in a more person centred way.

Supporting the learning of an individual with an autistic spectrum condition

You need to work hard at ensuring your understanding of the nature of someone's autism is as good as it can be. This is what will really enable you to appropriately support their learning. You are more likely to get the motivation right and also to be aware of the areas where they really do need to develop their skills as well as being supportive and delighted with the gifts and skills that they have. If an individual feels valued and that their interests and activities are respected they will be more prepared to face difficulties linked with change or learning new things, and also to accept the difficulties they have.

References and where to go for further information

References

Attfield, E and Morgan, H (2007) *Autistic Spectrum Disorders.* London: Paul Chapman Publishing

Department of Health (2009*) Valuing People Now: A New Three Year Strategy for People with Learning Disabilities.* London: Department of Health

Department of Health (2010) *Fulfilling and Rewarding Lives. The Strategy for Adults with Autism in England.* London: Department of Health

Hoy, R (2007) *Autism and me* (DVD). London: Jessica Kingsley Publishers

Welsh Assembly Government (2008) *The Autistic Spectrum Disorder (ASD) Strategic Action Plan for Wales.* Cardiff: Welsh Assembly Government

Websites

Autism Alliance www.autism-alliance.org.uk

Autism Cymru www.awares.org

National Autistic Society www.autism.org.uk

Scottish Autism www.scottishautism.org

Glossary

Asperger syndrome – Asperger syndrome is a condition on the autism spectrum named after Hans Asperger, who described it in 1944, the year after Leo Kanner published his observations. People with Asperger syndrome will have average or higher level intelligence and develop speech and language normally. However, they will have the difficulties in communication and social interaction that are experienced by all people with autism and may also have sensory difficulties.

Autism spectrum condition (autistic spectrum conditions) – autism is a lifelong developmental disability. The word 'spectrum' is used because whilst all people with autism experience difficulties in the same areas (they all have problems with communication, social interaction, ways of thinking and sensory processing), autism affects people in a wide variety of different ways. Those most severely impacted upon by their autistic spectrum conditions can be seen as at one end of the spectrum, whilst those who are able to function easily with little or no support can be seen as being at the other end of the spectrum.

Classic autism – another name for Kanner's autism.

Communication – the way that two or more people make contact, build relationships and share messages. These messages can be ideas, thoughts or feelings as well as information and questions. Communication involves both sending and understanding these messages and can be done through many different ways including speech, writing, pictures, symbols, signs, pointing and body language, for example.

Echolalia – the automatic repetition of words or phrases just spoken by another person. This can make somebody with autistic spectrum conditions appear to understand more than they really do.

High functioning autism – used to describe somebody who has autistic spectrum conditions, but who does not have a learning disability. This term is sometimes used as if it had the same meaning as Asperger syndrome.

Kanner's autism – used in recognition of the observations published by Leo Kanner in 1943. He was the first person to formally document the condition we now call autistic spectrum condition. Kanner identified all three parts of the triad of impairments as well as sensory processing difficulties.

Learning disability – includes the presence of a significantly reduced ability to understand new or complex information and to learn new skills together with a reduced ability to cope independently. A person's learning disability would start before adulthood, and it would have a lasting effect on their development.

Neurology – the area of medicine concerned with the diagnosis, research and treatment of disorders of the nervous system -- the brain, the spinal cord and the nerves.

Neurotypical – a term used to describe people who are not on the autism spectrum. The neurological development of neurotypical people is consistent with what most people would perceive as normal, particularly with respect to their ability to process linguistic information and social cues.

Person centred planning – used to describe placing the individual and their needs at the centre of planning any support they require. For somebody with autistic spectrum conditions this means focusing on the person but also on how their autism impacts on their life.

Pervasive developmental disorder not otherwise specified (PDD-NOS) – the term used to describe when someone has severe and pervasive impairments in all three parts of the triad of impairments but does not have autism.

Processing delay – commonly experienced by people with autistic spectrum conditions. It means they may take much longer than most other people to understand and digest spoken or written information or to answer a question.

Proprioceptive sense – our sense of knowing where we are in space, for example how we are able to judge getting through a doorway when carrying a large object. Many people with autism have sensory issues including with their proprioceptive sense.

Sensory issues – experienced by almost all people on the autistic spectrum, who very often process their senses differently or have problems with one or more of their senses. People with autistic spectrum conditions may find they are overwhelmed by one or more of their senses or they may seek sensory stimulation that appears excessive. The usual five senses (hearing, seeing, taste, touch and smell), as well as vestibular and proprioceptive senses, need to be considered when supporting somebody with autistic spectrum conditions.

The triad of impairments – three areas in which all people on the autism spectrum have difficulty; problems with communication, problems with social interaction and problems with ways of thinking and behaving.

Uneven cognitive profile – means people with autism have skills or talents in one area that are not consistent with their general level of ability. For example, somebody with autistic spectrum conditions and a learning disability, who cannot dress themselves or cross a road without help, may have a brilliant memory for remembering dates and the specific details of past events. Very occasionally the uneven cognitive profile includes an outstanding talent in one particular area, such as being able to draw to scale or play the piano to a very high standard.

Vestibular sense – our sense of balance.

Index